More Useful Words for Useless People

Robert Royal Poff

Cover Designer by Fabled Beast Design/ A.A. Medina

Cover Artist Atp_tupp

Edited and formatted by 360 Editing (a division of Uncomfortably Dark Horror).

Editor: Candace Nola

Contents

Dedication — IX

1. USEFUL WORDS FOR USELESS PEOPLE — 1

2. DAYLIGHT — 3

3. KISSING CANCER — 5

4. THERE IS NO JOY IN THIS — 7

5. HOW TO DIE YOUNG — 8

6. ICARUS — 11

7. ETERNALS — 13

8. YOLKS — 15

9. MERCURY — 17

10. RETROGRADE — 18

11. PLEASE LIVE FOR ME — 20

12. YOUR NAME — 22

13. 2D SCULPTURES — 23

14. CUBICLE KANYE — 25

15. 'TIL SHE WALK AMONG DEATH — 28

16. BOOTLEG KAFKA — 30

17. THE MISFORTUNES OF A MISCELLANEOUS MIND — 32

18. UNTITLED — 34

19. NOSTALGIC NOWADAYS — 35

20. LIPS — 37

21. ALL AT ONCE   39

22. VENUS   41

23. LAZY EYE   42

24. UNPROTECTED   44

25. IT'S ONLY SEX   46

26. TIDES   48

27. LOVE IS   49

28. U   51

29. FACTS WITH NO FACES   55

30. WHITE WALLS   57

31. THE SIMPLE MAN   59

32. TEMPLETON'S SPACEMAN   61

33. EARTH   63

34. ENDEARMENT   64

35. GENERATIONAL DISTANCE RACE   65

36. SHEAR THE MEADOWS   67

37. SKETCHBOOK SECRETS   69

38. INTO THE WILD   71

39. INTO THE CITY   72

40. MURAL   73

41. MURAL 2   76

42. COGNITOHAZARD   78

43. CARS WITHOUT MOTION   80

44. ZOMBIE   82

45. NEAR SIGHT, FAR   83

46. TANKS GONE EMPTY   84

47. MARS   86

48. BLOODLETTING   87

49. I, THE NONEXISTENT   89

50. TOMORROW   91

51. BUMPER STICKER PHILOSOPHIES   93

52. PANDORA'S BOX   95

53. BPD   96

54. TRAMPS LIKE US   98

55. LITTLE DEATH   99

56. THE VIOLINIST   101

57. UNTITLED   103

58. THOSE WHO WALK INTO THE TIDE   104

59. JUPITER   106

60. A SEXUAL ATTRACTION TO LIQUOR   107

61. QUOTING THE VILLAGE AND OTHER WAYS I SHOW I LOVE YOU   109

62. THE LOUDMOUTH KING   111

63. THE WALK   113

64. BUILD, BYPASS, BETRAY, REPEAT   115

65. UNIFORMED MUSICIAN   117

66. THIS IS AMERICA   119

67. POETRY   121

68. LIP RING   122

69. SCAR ON THE MOON   124

70. SALE ON HALF BAKED GRADUATES   126

71. SATURN   129

72. ROAD SIDE SOUL SALE   130

73. EMMA   132

74. CURLY   134

75. GLITTERING TRASH MOONS   135

76. BURIED AS A MAN (AN ODE TO BRIANNA GHEY)   137

77. AMERICAN DREAM   139

78. SELF SOUL COMMENTATION   141

79. ME AND HER AGAINST THE WORLD   143

80. MIRROR OF DAYS TO COME   145

81. FIREWORK FACELIFT   147

82. FOUR ARMS, FOUR LEGS, TWO FACE   149

83. FRAGMENTED   151

84. BEDS FOR PEOPLE FOR BEDS   152

85. URANUS   154

86. OTHER NAMES TO CALL ME   155

87. MY HAIR   157

88. STICK N' POKE   159

89. DOMINOES   161

90. CLOSE YOUR EYES AND LISTEN   163

91. DIFFICULT   165

92. UNINSPIRED CLOWN AT THE RAPTURE   168

93. OVERDOSE   170

94. THE CLUTTERED EMPTY   172

95. NO LOVER   174

96. MIDWEST OCCULTIST PLAYGROUND   176

97. CETACEAN STRANDING   178

98. HAIRCUTS AND RAZOR BLADES   180

99. SKIN SHEDDING   182

100. FREUDIAN SLIP   184

101. NEPTUNE   186

102. ANOTHER DISAPPOINTING PROSE   187

103. STARVED DESIRE   189

104. FIND ME   190

105. ADOPTED NAMES   192

106. TEN SECONDS BUILD FOREVER   194

107. A SELF AWARE SIMP'S STILL A SIMP   196

108. SOMETIME WE DIE   197

109. THE DIVINE FEMININE   199

110. UNTITLED 2   201

111. NOTHING LEFT BUT BURNING MEN   202

112. THAT WHICH ENDS   205

113. NIGHTLIGHT   206

114. About the Author   208

I dedicate this book to my mom, Kristy Poff, first and foremost, for shaping me into the person I am today. To my Aunt Joy, and Pap, William Poff, for always urging me forward when pursuing my dreams. To my Mama J, Jamie Blackhart, and my father, Joe Ortlieb, for never giving up on me. To my Nana, Phyllis Houska, for being my personal therapist during emotional times.

To all my siblings, DJ, Mena, Dharma, Raven, Phoenix, and Autumn, for being my pillars of happiness in an unforgiving world. To all my amazing friends, Faye Corbin, Logan Masenheimer, Emma Sites, and many more.

And to anyone who finds themselves in the need of the kinship of another broken, messy soul. I see you. I feel you. You are loved.

1

USEFUL WORDS
FOR USELESS
PEOPLE

I've stood in a house covering dead dogs and war whistles

I've stood on the graves of people

only remembered for the blocks

that desperately display their titles

I've stood in silence because

the hardest thing I've ever had to say

is I have no clue what to say

words are heavy unsaid

and heaviest unthought

reading further into texts you don't send

than the ones that you do

we're excited for a day that we don't know will come

so we rip out our eyes just to see what they'd look like

we found ourselves standing underneath the moonlight

our shadows constricted until the whole world was airtight

and though you died I lacked the skill to articulate

a remedy for death

how can I stop time with only these hands

what useless hands

I will not splatter words off a tongue that holds no value

I will not shed the tear off the mantle of a promise

I periodically pander to only when I'm the one who prospers

I've constantly paraded myself as a pariah

when I could no longer stand the presence of others

I claim my burdens as a singularity

like globe laden shoulders that lack the ambition I expire

you wasted death as I sit here wasting life

jotting useful words for useless people

2

DAYLIGHT

White hot jeans, or parachute pants

we can drive to New York popping percocets

in a manic panic, so we serve our best

attempt at acting confident

acting like we're not

each other's worst patterns

besides, behind every roll is a paradise

so lay under the stars with me

and guess which one's have yet to die

Schrodinger's coping mechanism

what doesn't kill me now

will only serve to harm me later

every tragedy so divine on the road to you

let me rest while I'm inside you

truly rest like I never could on my own

my hands Midas through your silk hair

spun grasp catching purpose for the first time

engraved between the grooves of your ribs

for now, stand on the edge of the world with me

watching time stop

chase my hand up abandoned roller coasters

and clench it once we've reached the top

fuck me on a railway

to the rumble of oncoming trains

and climax only when we've molded into one

and when they finally find out what's wrong with me

love me like it isn't there

3

KISSING CANCER

A doppelgänger of a monster

beyond that of any Lovecraftian

tale or conjure

that waggles its putrid form

an intermixed sleeper agent

that interjects itself within the

ranks of cell formation

of an unaware body

otherwise known to me

as mom

part of her anyway

an alien hiding under alias

of the woman I loved most

alienating her from the comfort of normality

thrusting her into path of cancers rampage

And I sat

I sat and quietly cried, knowing I could do nothing

holding a time bomb stitched into the inseam

of her very being

that kept us all on high alert

still I could do nothing but await the storm

And the dreams came

every night

a hex bag that grew with the insanity of sleepless night

and I kept a laugh track

continuously looping in my knapsack

hoping that vein humor would somehow

kill the indomitable beast

and possibly did

though more likely the treatment was the cure

Salvation was seen as the storm faded

the first day free of the foreign invader

and Death no longer spoke in seventeen syllable semantics

looming in a distance far too close

and cancer became a word

uttered only in my dreams

A dream that even now repeats

and a story told at sideways glance

as to never again

look into the eyes of the storm

4

THERE IS NO JOY IN THIS

The real beast lies right behind the eyes

in those swift beating frames of turnover

unveiling a captured nothingness

exposed to the world

The real beast lies buried deep

within the catacombs of glazed white

a deep emptiness unperturbed by your holy light

nor captured still within a land of waking grace

my real fear lies deep within the

great empty void

that momentarily consumed her

draining, pressing her body to the need for tubes

and belts and pylons

she rests

consumed by something more

5

HOW TO DIE YOUNG

First get the call

as your mother comes into work to get you

try to remain calm

as words like cardiac arrest and coding

permeate between sobs

try to reclaim the world

as it falls around you

as simple procedures evolve teeth of demonstrable ideology

Brace yourself for the fall

before the collapse to the floor

as your legs give out walking to the hospital

Gaze upon your family

sitting in a circle of chairs

tears, hurt, betrayal, threats at a God's vile hands

the first gathering in years

Hold in pain when you go back to see her

attempt to comprehend the machinery keeping her alive

the doctor's jargon echoing in your ears

the tubes in her throat, her veins, her bladder,

face the coma

whisper with a heart it takes to scream

and be no closer to piercing the veil that consumes her

Know that she died

know her current situation is much worse

that dying is worse in present tense

hold her hand but know there will be no reaction

Take her life upon you

make calculated decisions on how much torment

you're selfishly willing to put another life through

as her body systematically fails

with precision you couldn't dream possible

Hear those words

low chance of survival, the sickest in the hospital

ECMO machines, blood clots, amputation

watch her fade from the world

Know you weren't there enough

Think of all the fights

all the missed calls

all the chances not taken

Surround yourself with drowning bodies

mourn what used to be

watch her come back

grow hopeful

watch her fade

disappear within yourself

Hold on to anything to ground yourself

dream of funerals, live those dreams

start planning for the end

act like you can do that

grow tired of dying each time you look at her face

stop looking at faces altogether

laugh, don't forget to laugh

pretend to be human

Go to work

eat

sleep

breathe

all while she does none

Go out with friends

drink

smoke

claw your way out

hold on to everything with any semblance of anything

This is how you die young

6

ICARUS

If you were the sun,

honey, I'd die for just a taste

of something warm

honey, there is no sweeter place

though I carry this torch, I still worship your name

I could've sworn Hell would be easier than this

if someone begged me to stay

tell them I'd do it again

I'd take all the pain

just to feel you again

If you were the sun,

honey, my wings scorched by raze

when I defied the Gods with pendulous grasp

but words fall before you, deep and enchanting

and nothing breeds the fire like the sweet of your lips

from the first time you came, I realized why I never prayed

if someone begged me to stay

tell them I'd do it again

I'd take all the pain

just to feel you again

If you were the sun,

honey, I was born to feel your grace

no waking tongue could ever settle for another taste

no etterath, only salvation in your sweet embrace

giving up life for a single moment of living

when my wings could push no further

if someone begged me to stay

tell them I'd do it again

I'd take all the pain

just to feel you again

I'll love you more in all my future lives

I'll love you more in all my future lives

7

ETERNALS

I knew from the second I laid eyes on you

we'd never be eternal

since the very first date

that what you wanted far surpassed what I could give

knew that falling in love with you

would only lead to heartbreak

but I'd retread

I'd repeat

I'd endlessly recount

those limping footsteps just to do it again

all of it

every last second of every last fight

I'd have us break up a billion times

just to have loved you once

in every universe

in every timeline out there

I consistently

I persistently

choose you

a good thing doesn't stop being good

because it won't last forever

a beautiful piece of art is no less gorgeous

despite the fact that it'll decay

much like my memories

into tiny bits of snippets

so keep your time machine

I'd never use it to stop us

only to go back and love you all over again

for every second that I could

8

YOLKS

I extract the word emotion and jam it into abstract

a square cube shoved into multidimensional peg

counting all my chickens in one egg

yolk Picasso, coating house of neighborhood squabbler

scrambled off in getaway ride of runny ink

a dozen white catacombs wrapped in silicone enclosures

each concealing compact sun

perpetually breeding

the yolks, the yolks, the unfortunate jokes

cracked open and poured through forced open door

by man carelessly sacrificing predecessor of feathered swarm

but runny runs dry, just like a needle in pupilless eyes

drain out yolk like the pen drains the back of mind

which defines the porcelain spine, the endless twine

that constricts and mummifies any straight forward

brining of chicken's lives

filling vases with Da Vinci's runoff

just to turn around and mix it with some yolks

goddamn yolks, must be a joke

9

MERCURY

There are no scars to his flesh

nor perfections

he is a being of pure rejection

a prophetic pressure to surpass the past

a hero of a thousand tongues

that breathes in through paper lungs

a thousand unsung cries weigh his virgin heart

as he calmly circles

the great creator

IO

RETROGRADE

We should hit the road

and we should fall in love again

I know you're happy now

but we should fall in love again

we should hit the coast

and we should fall in love

we'd fuck, we'd get manic

we'd choke, we'd start to panic

now I smoke to get your taste off my tongue

now I drink to cover up the damage I've done

I was chasing pasts

you were running from

and we should fall in love

but objects in the mirror

are always closer than they appear

but my body in the mirror

never seemed quite so weird

we should fall in love

here I was falling in love

while you were falling apart

here I am looking for an ending

while you were hoping for a start

I was the dark side of an eclipsed moon

you were making lists of places

you'd rather see the setting sun

I see you're better off

and we should fall in love again

11

PLEASE LIVE FOR ME

She's at the bridge,

a silent voice

sponged within her useless skin,

it's bottled in, it's Vicodin.

There's endless numb encompassing

it's razor blades, it's under gaze

of imaginary center frame,

please live for me.

Her unkempt hair,

her eyes that dim with every stare,

she's in the air,

the koi's surround.

She's in the air,

the kois will drown.

She's more mute than words allow,

please live for me,

let me show you how to live.

12

YOUR NAME

I knew your name

far before any other

as if it had always been there

tattooed on my tongue

forever awaiting the day it could be used

to call out to you

13

2D SCULPTURES

I pity this miserable paper

for every word will be held down by its own meaning

every syllable tasked with sentiments words cannot achieve

words that supernova under their own weight

a weight graphite simply cannot grasp

no matter where I place these lines on the paper

no matter if I steal the "v" from "vicious" to create "victory"

or the "i" from "die" to represent myself

pressing my weight into the paper as it crafts

just words

I pity this miserable paper

all it will ever receive are words

only the skin of emotions that burrow through every mind

never admitting to its own passions

no music

no yearning beauty

no aching agony

just words

CUBICLE KANYE

Closed caption, fuck whoever's asking,

y'all slacking, face like DOOM but the mask skin,

his past kins wore rat skins,

first there was passion then ration,

so this is to the child that barrels past his predecessors,

and crafts his own Macaroni Mona Lisa's to last,

he's past patiently waiting to pass places,

so vast statements become accusations of fast paces,

when wunderkinds have reigned in divine signs for generations,

he tiptoes past curtsey, a young Morrissey,

and finds grandiose gestures inscribed in Cracker Jack boxes,

royal flush at the touch of kief,

two sun-bleached eyes in heat,

these artists can't keep their own pace,

flatfoot on a three leg race,

when writing is no longer a carbon copy cold case,

every poem just the deciphering of glyphs,

sprawled on waking skin,

he's impossibly hunting Shardik with a BB gun,

he's spitting fools' gold,

from canker sore to cotton mouth,

he'd load the gun but it's stuck in a hand and fist position,

backstory easily replaced with a chroma key,

cubicle Kanye, canonically deficient

of an incremental existence,

when years of Macaroni Mona Lisa game face,

has built up a tolerance to fame's grace,

breeding a generation hungry as Tarrare riding hunger strikes,

a writer whose sonnet mockings need margin coding to decipher,

his footnotes highlight chapters of McCarthy ever afters,

he's commonly after the point beyond perfection,

the glass ceiling can barely be a trampoline,

to these postmodern prodigies,

wordplay silhouette dances no longer hold a candle,

to past wordsmiths as uncanny as the lycanthrope in lederhosen scope,

now it takes a Cerberus bleating trilogies to match a single note,

the pacemaker perfections he follows,

tailing and hailing other perfectionists,

speed to matrix break,

it's no longer a bar rather a spiral of exponentially raised stakes,

crushing fates, stealing bread from plates,

so he triple knot the albatross,

when it takes its place,

and snakes around the sadder thoughts,

with growing trail that lag behind,

or triple dip the River Styx,

no tendon to mastermind,

he's sorta fine,

he sure to find

everything he does just to be,

the aching spine.

'TIL SHE WALK AMONG DEATH

She cups her hands to the moon,

always thirsting, always lusting for that last drop of light

her body's a prison to her desires

her teeth rip into the bleeding air

that avoids her lungs.

her teeth rip.

her lungs bleed.

she wails in the night.

her endless whispers grazing ears in gusts of wind.

her legs spread, her legs spread

ready for any stranger who will come to her false ideals

Tattoos, tattoos, tattoos

tattoos coat the stains.

so no one knows the past still wears her frame

wrapped in fresh tattoos that coat faded wounds.

and pills that no longer mask their true intent

her legs spread, her legs spread.

tattoos rip the skin,

her legs spread, an attempt to fend off the cicada shell of numb,

that collapses caustically into her skin,

she bends forward, whispering her love

into ears that no longer catch sound

her teeth rip, fresh tattoos bleed on her skin

she cups her hands to the moon,

burdened by a heavy nothing

16

BOOTLEG KAFKA

To me, you have always been poetry

a fearless pursuit in the eye of imperfection

clambering together enough parts to surpass

this mortal frame

To me, you've always been poetry

the cascading freedom of ensnaring the clouds

levitating in their wake

holding nothing to grasp everything

I read you between Kafka's lines

and worshiped you all the same

heard your voice echo within Hozier's ballads

soothing and tranquil standing as a grace of God

To me, you have always been poetry

an ax driven directly from my rock bottom

to my glass ceiling

To me, you are the universe

and everything it centers around

you are the quiet, and every sound that follows

loving you is a deeper sleep than death

as I curl up upon your deckled edge

sprawling out on layers of dripping ink

I will never be forced from

almost as if shackled to your great divine

but a poems never over

it simply

stops

17

THE MISFORTUNES OF A MISCELLANEOUS MIND

I was born a powerful soul eating up fragile skin

which dissolves and crumples to dust with every day

slingshot into an industry of giants

David against a room full of Goliaths

just another godless prophet proclaiming godly projects

it's unfortunate that the ones who create everything

are the ones that own nothing

my name exists as a ten letter numeric

you can hold on two hands

that conceals a desperate depression

I am a thousand stories stitched together

in an interconnected network of dueling

a gang war of idea dump, each struggling for survival

but trapped within single linear life

I'm nothing but the back of Bach's earshot

a perfect cannonball of life's cannon fodder

as poet dies and enters Robin Williams' filmography

a cinephile with desperate desire to be great

you'll grow up counting pennies if you grow up counting blessings

so I backpaddle in the wake of Aesop Rock

and pick at Poe's passion

to posterize any idea that happens by

rip the epic inner struggles of Beowulf

from camp of creative concentration

to climb Mt. Olympus and gander

at the grandeur of fulfillment

I was born an oracle of death and the bringer of lives

18

UNTITLED

You don't have to love me

the entire time we're alive

just promise you'll hold my hand

as I die

and pretend you always did

19

NOSTALGIC NOWADAYS

I used to spend my days duel venturing

single player games

blissfully unaware of the problems in the backdrop

now I spend my days jotting thoughts

that cleanse the towers halls

dusting off the master's Nobel's

in the hopes of one day achieving half their glory,

a clergyman with a mental orgy den

a forgery of a young Morrissey

until the flora crowned citizens start singing

"your princess is in another castle now"

and I begin the expansion of genocidal takeover

to bounce off the cranium of every tortoise

and collect coins from the hardship

of smashing fists against the hovering pavement

never to find the damsel I venture so carelessly for

I used to spend my days

binging a consumption of as many cartoons

as I could stomach

now I face Scooby-Doo-esque spooky adventures

unmask anxiety held within culprit of terrorizing poltergeist

or assimilated into the daily nothings of the protagonist's parents

I used to explode with imagination

injecting full length epics into plastic figurines

which has now evolved into words

that harbor an entire existence of their own

the most oddly shaped universe graft

branded on topological maps of graphite mountains

LIPS

She remains fixed as the top jaw

outspoken as the bottom

born in roots of similarity

like teeth that smile a dazzling yellow pageant dream

coated in cavity formations

that she cherishes for breaking conformity

crooked lean as she forces from sea froth line

She carries fire lips to funnel pipe dreams

a shut mouth catches no pulitzers

so she screams her ideals

honey mouthed

flooding tales straight from the horse's informant

not bothering oblong smile when quiver lip catches

so she bleats her dreams

loud enough to make up for mouth's lack of twinship

She was born with silver spoon fillings

expelling bombastic ideals that bypass plum's blockage

her mouth filled with dynasties desperate for harvest

bazooka tooth, grenade tongue

pull the pin when the days done

21

ALL AT ONCE

In that single moment that you smile

a thousand stars combust in a brilliant cosmic dance

a bird surrenders itself to fate

spiraling groundward, its wings extended

a moth dies, drowned in the wool of a lamb

the Earth spins, carelessly altering the position of billions

as it forces its way closer to the sun

a writer crafts his masterpiece

while his roommate hangs in the other room

legs still twitching above a knocked over chair

millions of campfires illuminate huddled families

gorgeous, hand stoked jewels, cascade down the boundless

curves of a models chest

flaring under the clatter of cameras

fireworks glaze over the eyes of the blind

music crashes like wings over the deaf

everything, everywhere

moving

existing

fighting for attention, all at once

yet still the most important thing to happen

in that microcosm of a second

is your smile

you are everything the universe strives to be

22

VENUS

She lightly speckles the child in leeches

a ritual brought forth from the sky

for the sky, to the sky

purified in leeches

a face of just eyes

that consumes the horrors

brought forth by aliens wearing similar skin

love sprouts from the child

as does hate

the markings of the damned

briefly lit before the flames of rigid sun

LAZY EYE

T-shirt long enough to craft a mobile home with

baggy jeans a street mop when the rain shift

mismatched beanie she got for Christmas

to cloak an unwashed maw of hair

her knapsack a dilapidated cataract toned package

tooth twisted third from the left to break formation

and her imperfections she sees as immovable impressions

but she'd be nothing without that lazy eye

Never been one to bow out gracefully

hastily provide a quick escape to the vacancy

a brain that curves sharply to the abstract

and mystifies overseers as she shoegazes

whips from Gatsby in a gawsy

to a sheets persona inflicted with centric melodrama

a case of overindulgence in oppression

as her scars add a need to please

and her imperfections she sees as impoverished implications

but she'd be nothing without that lazy eye

The warm and subtle aftertaste

her lips left as they grazed my face

a body tattooed with past stories

she thought I had what it took to be happy

I knew I never stood a chance

but she never stopped trying

twin lightning rods hiding from the storm

trying to take up the same place

in a dual one-sided relationship

but she'd be nothing without that lazy eye

24

UNPROTECTED

All sex is unprotected

as I run my grip across your throat

an act of primal dominance

feigning for a showcase of love

All sex is unprotected

run streaks down my back with dirty nails

until the polish chips into my skin

make me bleed, feel me bleed

all so that the wounds cover the scars

all sex is unprotected

you taste like jazz and cigarettes

and I'm too obsessed with you to ever love myself

everything from your iridescent smile

to the way you buck your hips as you cum

I'm obsessed with you

baring the full brunt of my blistering devotion

to your flesh

All sex is unprotected

I stand before you prepared to lose a part of me

I know I'll never be able to retrieve

just to briefly forget where my body ends

and where yours crashes around it

a beast with two backs

blossomed in an unfathomable display

IT'S ONLY SEX

Press my back into the car seat

as I crash into you like a drunk driver

more a seizure than an act of pleasure

it's only sex

Looking up at you beaded with sweat, thinking

you'd look so much better with my hands around your throat

it's only sex

But the ending of a universe happens

like fireworks crashing through intermolecular space

as friction pushes our bodies closer

a fight against nature to truly touch for the first time

it's only sex

Fall in love with me, it'll make the hookups sweeter

but it's only sex

No wonder all art is the product of addiction

as I close my eyes

feeling your body hungrily pulsate around me

knowing this is the closest either of us will get to God

it's only sex

26

TIDES

From my point of view

there isn't a single grain of sand

in any ocean that doesn't

crave your touch

with each passing wave

27

LOVE IS

Love was always a

broken

stained state with no center

desperately clinging, barely holding it together

something I had to chase down

in an endless hunt for some sort of salvation

love was always a hunt

a fever, a dream, a fluttering single second with an aching

lust to follow

Love was always you

though I didn't know that

before I even knew your name

I found you in the pills

I found your laughter in poetry

your smile in the stars

Love was just a word with silent letters

pronounced as the wind whimpers

but caught its syllables in your eyes

and formed its first real sentience from the backbone of lust

crafted into some unfathomable display

Love has always proclaimed its lovecraftian grandeur

carefully carving a vessel in your form

28

U

Cause you can fuck me

up, over, or loving if you don't mind

me wanting to stay over

you make my highs feel sober

and my sobers so incredibly high

I'll never hurdle

you make my Earth turn

on an axis I never even thought possible

and other cliches I had thrown away

to the dismay of past partners

From the moment I exploded

into untimely being

somewhere crushed between the seams of living and nonliving

forced to breath

I had this need to please the world

a lovers casualty

and it wiggled and fell from me like a loose tooth

which wouldn't be the first time I'd lose a part of me

for surgery, for psychology

for when they left with my first heart attached so carefully

to the beat up back seat

the parts I didn't keep

and the rusty fender falling off my car

reminds me more of me

Cause you can fuck me

up, over, or loving if you don't mind

that I'll never ditch my worse side

from the blind side

of my car window

as I

speed

past my insecurities

trying to ignore what was constantly building

But me just sitting there thinking

if you got a new body every seven years maybe I'd

eventually get one attractive enough

to get one of the pretty girls to love me

a dream that proved true when you found me

cause all I wanted from a young age

was the love I could never give myself

cause inside my heart was just as ugly

but grade school sweethearts swooned from time to time

and I regret to tell you that I never grew to love me

Cause you can fuck me

up, over, or loving if you don't mind

that one day I'll probably end

what is all of mine

if I can't get these lovely little thoughts of death

out of my broken stuffy head

Since I found you I've been starting to reclaim my past

some things I haven't been able to do in a while

like look in the mirror for more than those dreaded few seconds

when I get out of the shower before I find the disdain in my reflection

and a new taste in music

that's a

sweet and tranquil habitat

or my eyes that seem just a

tad

bit

less

boring

brown

even though they're probably still just the same

and your eyes always look more unique on you anyway

Cause you can fuck me

up, over, or loving if you don't mind

I dream of one day not needing you

so I can have you freely

I dream of one day holding you

without my insides screaming

about how breakable you are

about how good I am at breaking

things when I grip them a bit too tight

and get a bit too high or a bit too loud

but I will fuck you

only ever lovingly

as if it's all I was made to do

29

FACTS WITH NO FACES

You still cross my dreams

even after enough years have passed

that I barely remember your voice

watching your lips move

a tempest dance to spite lesser gods

that twirled around your smoke and mirrors

so even after I wake

your touch lingers in caustic bliss

cause you had NPD

and I had BPD

a match made in crossword puzzles

so let's intersect in ways we were always meant to

in April you told such sweet lies

left me stranded until May

but even the perfect lover

wouldn't change the fact I can't change the facts

so I'm not looking to fall in love

I'm just searching for something else

to replace that beating rhythm

you took when you left

30

WHITE WALLS

Everywhere around me are white walls

trapping, consuming, pressing against me at all times

concealing me within their grasp

forcing me down a worn road so many have tread upon

white walls brought forth by others

no color, no life to their face

no reason for being except to keep me

the mouse, from reaching the cheese

even after I have won, I've won the goal of another

won the game of the white walls

while without knowing being kept from my own

I am everyone, representing the gifted, representing the not

perceived as the tree hanging from a rocky cliff

such struggle in its survival,battle-scarred it lacks the chance to bear fruit

a tree, weather battered and bruised bark, battle-scarred

breaking its way to chance, hidden beneath the soil

given the opportunity to break through these white walls,

open blind man's eyes for the first time

tumble the white walls that had so confined, marking my own path

no longer certain I'm heading in the direction of the cheese

certain if I may be so lucky to find it

that I am not the many brought into the realm of the white walls

31

THE SIMPLE MAN

The simple man is the extraordinary man's cousin

and the ordinary man's brother

and the something something to another

hurling hate at mother's face

because she didn't breed him designer genes

and he screams

screams because there is nothing left to do

screams to ward off the void that threatens consumption

screams because it's the only working function

screams because any sound is better than silence

always silent

always desperate

always yearning

always dreaming

never seeing

always question

always hope

always try

never one to break the glass ceiling

so he suffocates within his own purpose

always praying for the torture of the lament to come

32

TEMPLETON'S SPACEMAN

Robert Thomas Poff

three names all heralded by those before

yet that hold no weight today

no merit nor badge of honor

I am named after the forgotten

for the forgotten, and to be

myself, forgotten

I am everyone

for everyone's the same

all heading down a worn path

chisel in hand, hopeful that heir carvings remain

yet, the walls once again become bare

eroded by a world lapsed in repeated amnesia

a world too consumed in advancing

to keep aware of all its identities

yet, perhaps, this road holds more than me alone

holds Robert, holds Thomas

visible for a split second just beyond the shoulder

of offhand photographs

a lineage of my own spacemen stand in pose

a Russian nesting doll of spirits

33

EARTH

I am the corroded rock on which he stands

crumbled under blistered feet

that taints the fresh patch of snow

waxen as the bones it holds,

far from the path foreseen

as the drunk tramples forth

his eyes dulled by artificial Glaucoma

that has been injected into his mind

cataracts spawning as he further deteriorates

still planting fruit in the wake of his conquest

34

ENDEARMENT

I stand not on the pedestal of love

but eye it down on a swivel chair of disaster

a noose, noticeably loose, entrapping

constricting constantly faster

a fanatic for speeding life's race, tempting fate

tempting freefall, no parachute to parade

with an irate stare

gaze gradually into cyclops eye

yellow glow at the end of tunnel resides

courageously courting the corridors of your soul

or coordinates of combined constellations

but arms unable to escalate to levels

high enough for stars to notice

so here I sit behind robots eye

daydreaming under the stars

35

GENERATIONAL DISTANCE RACE

Constantly comparing myself to my predecessors

continuously coming up short

not even a contestant in my own rat race

the moldy McGuffin of cheddar

that awaits within the labyrinth of supernova'd blackstar

paired with the pale man, and endless pendulum

just a photocopy of a photocopy

of a never-ending domino chain of watered down ideology

I just want to be great

as greedy as it is to say

I don't want to leave this world the same

I'm drowning in a cluster of limbs

a Dante-esque fever dream of claustrophobia

a cynic is only as good as his arsenal

hoisted by Diogenes and drug to the center of the room

where he shouted

"Plato, I have found your man"

a contest which predates the Gregorian calendar

handpicked and chosen for a select cult of culprits

since man held flame in hand and conquered

left the animal kingdom completely bonkers

and I?

I'm simply an occupation of space for the time being

I just want to matter

I'm scared of a word, I'm scared of a line

I'm scared of the passing of time

but when the eyes stare, the only eyes, I fear are mine

36

SHEAR THE MEADOWS

Words fall deftly at your touch

to compromise majesty with insatiable rust

the wild vineyards in your eyes

to prosper sight from stye

it's not the distance, it's what's behind

there is no obstacle to pass, just the bitter last

like secrets sworn in meadows of broken glass

there is no head in looking back

it's not of matter, it's a fact

and if the skies ever lit with sanctified word,

it shrank to your dark and glorious form

that kind of loves been battered by the past

like a ground that is giving

like a mark on a sword

like erosion of soil after bountiful storm

arose from the tomb, like a flower that's born

I watched you grow a name

I pierced a vein

and bled into your swarm

37

SKETCHBOOK
SECRETS

Life is nothing but a series of doodles in my sketchbook

scratchy lines evolving into horrific beasts

happy little figures, or scattered thoughts half formed

lacking conformity to break each others thoughts

some never to be completed, the hand that feeds them never to return

others take over great amounts of space

consuming all until there's no end to their expanse

before you know it, there's nothing but doodles

stacking each other, fighting desperately to be noticed

a dizzying wave of confusion with more parts than any map

eraser shavings sprinkle wounds that will never truly fade

no matter how hard they're rubbed out

and just when it seems as if the paper will burst

the next page is revealed

blank and lifeless

restlessly awaiting creation

more monsters, more happy figures, more illusions of blind imagination

spring up

clashing violently but coming together in a dazzling firework of lines

that's all life is

lines

a vast array of patterns

yet still simply lines

INTO THE WILD

Wunderkind turn wanderlust

turn Supertramp to pinch the bus

and lift the shadowed naked us

walking towards the couch

but I was heading for the coast

just a willing, winter ghost

to curb the still tongue of nature

that ever beats within a foreign frame

it's hard to coerce a forced future

even easier to defy expectations

into the wild

let the memories flow through me

let the memories turn to lust

INTO THE CITY

Blunderbuss turn bandersnatch

consume the parts that tippy-tap

I've seen my mom wear suits and tired eyes

don't hesitate to buy my web

compensate me for enabling my addictions

in a starved box of bricks

to kill the vapid eyes of nature

who will never feed an industry standard

it's hard to claim fake skin

even easier to accept it

into the city

let the memories evaporate

we will all become memories

MURAL

We're nothing but folktales

desperados in coattails, swinging life by the palm

trees chopped to storyboard manifestos

for when all of us are gone

but to be gone is to be replaced with what's beyond

so when you're successful

are you a made man or life's maid then

guess that all depends on who made them

and whose left to rise in the morn

but not mourn like the gravewatcher's scorn

more like drained moonshine in his cup

as sun pivots in continuous loop

not loop like the tied noose window

poems tend to stick their heads through

but loop like the inside of the hula hoop I'm thrown for

I prefer my wars fought in word form

I prefer to shake spears not draw swords

that man at arms drawn by armless man

gazing at the stars

that avant-garde to mirror mural of Jaco's halls

Jericho, so when bombs blow

build bomb shelters out of stitched memory

diptych, compiled manuscripts of Sisyphus styled daily war

where war is not fought armed with gun

but rather exponentially sold to highest bidder

illegal arms race to a finish line that isn't real

victory ribbon rod draws in for meal

and not meal like a minute made ordeal

more so a prime staple of rubber zeal

but not stable, concentration camp for metaphorical horses stable

allowing instead for horses to graze freely on maple

and not prime like Optimus

or humanoid goliath of any kind

rather brought up to level where would be his eye

prime like the point in life where you reach that high

and high like vicodin arm wraps

strangling blood pressure cuffs

on bathroom floors, laying on the places where we lie

we're nothing but folktales

spam emails, and intricately woven network

of junk found within neighboring trench warfares of yard sales

just fractals hidden inside plain squares

but most of all

wooden figurines devoured by endless whales

41

MURAL 2

We're nothing but rat kings

Boltzmann brains with impromptu fruition lanes

Ouroboros chains of endless rat king remains

when inspiration came, like Adam into Eve

or strikes like a bat to the knees

who plead for just a drop of creative lead

or lean, anything you're sipping to chemically alter needs

but a high horse is no worthy steed

nor stolen valor, somehow starving the beast with feed

carnivorous

canker sores and deliverance

and one too many deaths pile up like prerequisites

cheaper tricks like how to make the self unexist

I'm busy trading riddles with the exorcist

wordplay go from blitzed to shamanist

I'm nothing but an ear to twist

an iron fist, mummified in velvet mitt

or smitten to the 10th degree

who permafrost your chemistry

and drop your dexterity

to a step below the pedigree

no Stranger Things in memory

it's sounding like a D in D

there is no lyrical comprehensivity

in a rabbit hole dipped fantasy

like you and me, in sonder reality

like TV, like IV of codeine in the 40s

more six steez, like Drake T's

we're nothing but MP3s burned on nameless DVDs

subtleties, a desperate need to please

and among many others, a grandiose disease

of Ice Cube's and Eazy-E's

but most of all

better than our previous selves

like a cicada

peace

42

COGNITOHAZARD

We're sitting on an abandoned bridge

and I'm thinking about the gap between your teeth

that breaths uniqueness into your captivating smile

and the gap between your fingers

ones I so boldly wish to plug with my own

to save a sailing ship from a fate

it was never in any danger of

I'm thinking about anything but the gap between us

I already rashly proclaimed "I love you"

now I'm lingering in those final few seconds

while you're mulling over what to say

taking comfort in the fact

you haven't spoken yet

so there's still that chance you could love me back

it's irrational, I know it's irrational

you've already said you're not looking for what I am

but every poem has been translating

to thinly veiled attempts to capture your laugh

my racing thoughts keep pounding back to

cognitohazard

and how there's a certain beauty in not knowing

these precious few seconds

where the cats still in the box

neither dead, nor alive but some third state

that transcends the bounds of mortal frame

we're sitting on an abandoned bridge

and instead of thinking about diving off

instead of the gap between me and the ground

I'm jumping into proclamations

confessions to close that gap between us

43

CARS WITHOUT MOTION

60

We broke down

somewhere along a long drive

instead of watching stars

we watched the gas deteriorate

huddled in to keep the cold out

still it was the day I finally felt young

70

We broke down

somewhere along a long drive

in my sunset red Camry

the baggage of past trips resting in ashy coffee grains

stained into the dash where your feet would rest

the fender scratched from when you drove high

still it was the day it felt right to be alive

80

We broke down

somewhere along a quiet street

baby pack your bags, bring a sweater cause it's cold out

we'll sleep on the floor, catching fireflies to keep the dark out

finally afford the cracks beneath our feet

90

Get out the car

100

Get out of the car

110

Let's ruin each other's lives

at the ripe old age of adolescence

120

We broke down

somewhere along a long drive

and though I never stopped loving you

we picked up

somewhere after a long while

130

But nothing's ever finished...

it just stops

0

ZOMBIE

I was born a paradox

immediately before my first breath

before life had reached my ears

Death quivered, wearing black hole eyes which consumed

I was born the same way a star dies

one iridescent blast followed by the cold vastness of space

I was born the way a song ends

I was born

never created

and it was, in rebirth

I came to find myself existing

in a shell I didn't want

on a rock that didn't want me

cast into a second rock of blind mock divine

NEAR SIGHT, FAR

Look beyond the veil of near sight, far

out to that which, gone unseen, has thrived

untouched and as so untamed by minds before

unreigned and unthrottled in their roams, power untapped

and bear with you as you cross the veil

a rope to ensnare thought at its most violent form

the thought of new given way to by experiences of old

in full glow of moonlight path

within large vacant nothing only perceivable by you

and look with near sight, far

off into the other world's awakened slumber

46

TANKS GONE EMPTY

I'm running out of ideas

the ink just isn't taking to the paper

as I mate the two together

perhaps my dreams will never be bound in leather

maybe if I could staple my thoughts down

before they mature into flight

mend my life with concrete

instead of staring down the barrel of an eraser

maybe then I could make up for lost time

staring at failed origami crumpled meteorites

trying to suit up each line with rhyme

injected with reason like heroin needle

conjure up as many scriptures as limited breath will allow

try to perspire emotion, but ending up words

from the mouth of others spoken

I can't even pick up the pen, it's too heavy

just like my eyes, they won't remain steady

it's half past 2am and I haven't slept in days

but the dormant words awoken

the only thing that guides the hand on

is a far off tomorrow when a child resting upon

the wake of Death's chase picks up my book

to escape life's unpassable plunder

just one soul is all it takes

to keep a pyromaniac mind from running asunder

pray be me that they come to elucidate

just follow the pied piper into precious paradise plunder

MARS

The butcher circles the sacred cow

dripping leeches onto its exposed heart

beating, impossibly beating, as it pulls apart

separated by two plants that intertwine

the pulsing atriums, stunting the rushing blood

the man's black hole eyes consume

no longer observing but correcting

twisting red greed over the canvas

BLOODLETTING

Alarm clock licking loops

cement bedsheets encapsulating

my body like Pompeii statue stand

and leeches devour festering skin but I no longer care

Slip coma like back to squeezing slumber

a flatliner to see how long I can remain

concealed, entirely hidden from him

he who pours leeches on my flesh but I no longer care

A cotton capsule swallows my head

a systematic reducer of life's noise

I bleed onto sheets, but he no longer cares

he who ritualistically endows me in the voodoo leeches

I lay, chained, rigor mortis setting in

as I wait for the perfect chance to rise

the sun floods in but reason remains absent

infected blood drained through portly leeches, but I no longer care

A mirrored man as he enters the room

and leeches devour festering skin, but I no longer care

49

I, THE NONEXISTENT

I am not a poet

to be a poet would be to exist as my own entity

I am the poem

I am my work

I am nothing more

I am not a writer

I am the catalyst of lost art

thrust haphazardly into every atom of my soul

I am not a man

nor do I bear any resemblance to one

I am cogs, and belts, and metal pylons

I am my stories

I am nothing else

I am not an artist

though I wear the false face

tearing at the slapped together seams

I am seventeen syllables of sleepless nights

I am an endless waking void

always so cluttered in its emptiness

I am my work

I am nothing else

50

TOMORROW

I have got to be seen to be felt

to be heard, before speaking a word

I have got to be seen to feel

to be torn, at the inseam

stitched down my porcelain spine

and strung out, sinews dripping

for mock crows to guzzle

still pulsating, still pirouetting in the breeze

I have got to be seen to cease starvation

to tote endlessly, Sisyphus rock to plummet daily

please someone come and touch me

with limelight, beyond musical queries

and prove to myself I'm still corporeal

in this shambled, illustrious mess of a frame

I have got to feel some day

I keep telling myself that

maybe tomorrow

maybe something

51

BUMPER STICKER PHILOSOPHIES

I could print out all my life's beliefs

gift them a fancy font, vividly colored

and portrayed through an image

slap my bumper sticker philosophies to a car

and give drivers insight to my life as they go by

I could speak on page with full devotion to the written word

allow people to graze its face value as they skim shelves of others teachings

all the same, leather bound or cheaply crafted, all the same

I could paint a dozen works of art

each with more immaculately spoken truths than the last

but all it amounts to is one bumper sticker philosophy after the next

one discount Democritus preach after another

all of it only adding to a quote worthy of a few inches on the rear of a car

my words crave more

they excel in greed and refuse to be stuck as one of the others an old book whose pages are caked shut with dirt

a bumper sticker partly washed away from years of wear and tear

no my words crave greatness

yearn achievement

and lust power

a bumper sticker philosophy too dangerous to wear for fear of distracted crashes

---

PANDORA'S BOX

It's not that you invented poetry within me

it's that before you there was nothing

no beauty, no pain

no dark, no light

stagnant

you were my big bang

and I've attempted to mold the cosmos ever since

so it's not that I'm incomplete without you

it's that there is no me without you

you were my spawning

and all the same, you will be my end

BPD

Stop me not, but let me jog

folly work turn failed to fog,

I'm nothing but a mesh of cogs

capturing the clashing will between

intuitive and spectrum.

We can send a ship to Mars,

but can't fix what's wrong inside my head,

and all my heroes pop prescriptions

so that orange bottle must be a miracle of beautiful visions

couldn't see past the visions,

speckling the walls until the car drove off the cliff,

I wish that it didn't

but wishing doesn't make a difference,

tugging guillotine smokescreens,

packaged neatly in a need to please

twisted dialect go Worf Effect.

I talk in twists to unfurl my tongue,

obscure meaning because I'm too scared

to share the truth about me,

borderline, the only time, I slap five with the one percents.

I'd notice your red flags

if I didn't have my own to look through,

I just wanna feel, but still so heartless,

it's simple and clean

but it's not me.

I hate art more beautiful than mine,

just like I hated her for getting over me,

before I could consider moving on

cause she was the best drug I've found thus far,

abusing everything I ever knew,

am I abusing your love?

I wish I knew,

perhaps I'm feeling like I need something new,

because you decided you needed someone new,

overdose before I ever touch a prescription,

addicted to everything I ever came across,

run circles around my potential,

guess that's why I always relapse,

the cloven hooves of Death's pale horse reflect prescription dinners,

but so do winners.

I should've seen the signs before the signs became the better times,

you're the most, my mind-

TRAMPS LIKE US

I once fell asleep on a sinking corpse

coddled by their lingering warmth

as I attempted just once to sleep through the night

listening to the faint echoes of heartbeats,

that pressed my ears like symphonies

a long forgotten comfort of a child swaddled

now you are the space between her eyes

and the blood between her lips

the vast space between constellations

that exists in only your gravitational pull

sunk into my self preservation cleverly disguised as love

I never loved you, but I'm good at feigning such emotions

so good I've convinced myself I could love you

I once fell asleep on a sinking corpse

embedded into the grooves of her skin

with such coherency, it's almost horrifying

maybe if we had just kissed at another time

LITTLE DEATH

Please marry me in the back of my mind,

let's play make believe,

make mountains out of medication,

and pretend we aren't too fucked up

to ever truly be together,

switching from I was born to love you

to I will live to hate you,

is too bitter to believe.

Please marry me in the back of my mind,

far away from obtrusive hands,

hands that turn Midas at your touch,

we traded small deaths for smaller sparks,

anything to feel

but you made me feel like long drives,

cigarette smoke, and just getting by

cruising down I-95,

sober had never felt so high.

Please marry me in the back of my mind,

sit on the rooftop and count the days away,

there must be tens of thousands of them,

I hope they're easy

but things are never easy, so the only thing I can hope for is that

when it gets so breezy, that our sailboats can't find safety,

I hope we get stranded in the same alignment and float out to sea together.

56

THE VIOLINIST

She stands stage high cradling life's deadliest weapon

like an extension of her own throat

in such a way that made speech primitive

the world stopped

halted millions of years of pushing to listen

she stood there, entirely secluded

in an existence utterly her own

tempest fingers performing a duet with the string

as much a war march as a ballet

her glazed eyes might as well not exist

every sense repurposed, plowed into every note

that walloped the crowd of onlookers

dispersing their every thought

mindlessly tracking her frantic wails

she shook in tune with her own mental Mozart

swaying soundlessly, foot tapping morse

the crowd gasped needlessly

any offstage sound already dimensions behind her

she bounced between allegretto and allegro

claiming both as her own

the world only began again with the final discharge

of her maple sword

UNTITLED

I excel at surpassing these t's when I'm crossing lines

and dot my i's with cyclops eyes

slice with scythe inside fish hook q

but still slide my words into perpetual nothingness

swallowed by a reluctant susurrus

resting perpendicular to a palindrome

of backwards melancholy Ferris wheel

trying to sound mature but coming off childish

toting a pistol with metaphor magazine

but still children's games, blast toys,

no recoil, no exploits, all rise crescendo

squirt gun held level with bank robber eyes

steal from the alphabets verses

to rearrange into my own constellations

THOSE WHO WALK INTO THE TIDE

So I see you've started smoking

and other things I've noticed

in the gap between when we spoke

exploding whale balloons

that breached the soil just to drown

boot theory

as one taps the ground the other follows

so when you caught the chute

I hit the latter

so I see you started smoking

cut your hair and changed your name

like you killed the you

that included me

but your names still a sleeper cell

and nothing's further than

the view from halfway down

cause she's the type of girl all songs are about

and I'm the type all movies are made for

so just think of the art

they could've made about us

so I see you started smoking

so at least I live on in our self destruction

fuck a lucid dream

we did it all to feel awake

we will always be

those who walk into the tide

JUPITER

He trots barefoot over the decay laden soil

sinking into the ground

standing on air, drowning in air

devouring himself

Ouroboros ring shackling

desperately seeking a second face,

to cultivate deeper emotions

guided only by the wind

that howls nicotine spells through his hair

A SEXUAL ATTRACTION TO LIQUOR

He says hello with his tongue down my throat

goodbye with his grip down my thigh

tube slides and hair dye

breakfast in bed and morning-after pills

drama queens and movie scenes

he likes his darkness fed

and he tastes like nicotine

his ivory skins my ketamine

and the foundation of all human suffering

rests in the creases of his lips

He was a martyr to my perfection

no wonder I still pen lies about him

but I never liked him

I fetishized him

ran dope deals when I was inside him

trading white for green

and every hue in between

in a wild exhibit of blind will

wanting every past lover

to linger in the taste of the supplementary pressure

of a heated soul

carved haphazardly to plug

the cracks of his dripping soul

he says hello with his grip on my throat

goodbye with his tongue down my thigh

61

QUOTING THE VILLAGE AND OTHER WAYS I SHOW I LOVE YOU

I can vaguely recall

the smell of your leather jacket

when we first kissed

the thought that this was the feeling

I had been searching for my entire life

when the world finally

abruptly

went quiet

all those voices in my head just seemed to

dissipate

in one moment I was enough for this world

even if a million moments later it might kill me

for now I was enough

you were the quiet, a ship

slowly sinking into the ocean

the world moves for love

kneels before it in awe

62

THE LOUDMOUTH KING

I don't mean to get prolific

when I slam my finger in the door

I don't mean to get specific

when my emotions go on tour

This agony proceeds me through the door

and doesn't even have the courtesy to say thank you

as I hold it open

sinking into susurrus splatters like nothing really matters

damn

just a loudmouth king preaching from phantom pedestal

like all this belly achings going to stop my belly aching

got a sliced thumb

running around like this paper cut is a fight won

like there's some sort of victory in a day done

like all my poetic epics aren't just jest fun

slipping back into safety of empty vowels

violating any sense of privacy

because I'm just a loudmouth king

expelling rhetoric like they're the lost amendments

And if knowledge is money,

then how come I can't trade in these

folk tales for a little wealth

because if I'm a dime a dozen

then the only thing I'll have to fear is fear itself

63

THE WALK

The walk began, deadpan, should've been a dead man

with the rest of the squad tangled around mangled ankles

tugboat trooping behind the makeshift commander

all lost souls trailing me so today I am Christ

Jesus, I wish they didn't leave us

bullet riddled

faced the fates with uncanny valor

I couldn't preserve a soul but my own

possibly not even that

left behind to bleed out, as my cicada shell continued forth

and to quote he Sixth Sense "I see dead people"

every time I close my eyes, which keeps them wide

a solo trip green mile

limping lead grazed, a wounded animal

slingshot a rock salt slug back at any alien life forms

I came across

how do I go to war when wars on the go?

war is in the soul, guess that's why they call us soldiers

a river opens before me, and crimson closes behind

I'm looking for God, but I'm not seeing sights

as eyes betray, dripped into a void of black tar

the sand becomes a bed

guardian angel turns to assailant

as cold metal licks forehead, and barrel looms

a melancholy lightning bolt awaiting orders

but death is not yet exhaled

rather hoarded as the walk continued once more

a loop of footsteps with no clear direction

and a thunderous cannon always awaiting its correction

64

BUILD, BYPASS, BETRAY, REPEAT

Something wicked this ways born

from the tongue of a God whose flaked to the Earth

with the shake of the ground

and the roar of the dirt

drops a poison, packed in Eldritch

in a grandiose expression of Pandora's box

a buzzard roosted shoulder sends the chip into despair

and scientists split atoms before they split hairs

there is no honor among these pansy picking hooligans

that never stopped to wonder if they should

when the Jurassic tethers dribble Death in the purest state

Boy sours

fights the oppression of powers

stares over Cronenberg blueprint for hours

weighing his devotion against his will to stay man

trying to rebrand Prometheus' gift like it was his own pleasantries

the enemy passes to the final lap

the time has come to act or snap

so they crop circle ants just to Minotaur their paths

as paper tigers print the hand of God

the bystanders watch

not a gasp or applause

as compact sun mourns mushroom clouds,

from the mouth of a boy who's lost all but his tongue

I, myself, have become Death, destroyer of worlds

65

UNIFORMED MUSICIAN

When I was a boy, I dreamed of being a musician

feeling the twang of the guitar in my hands

screaming fans bellowing chants,

raising their arms in Nazi like devotion

and so when I was drafted, I dreamed

An Ak47 became my guitar

shredding its keys and blasting a melody so bold,

strap over my shoulder as I waltz the battlefield

the crowd loved it

damn, did they scream

screamed and barked for their comrades to tune in

as I lit the air

and so as I killed, I dreamed

Only twelve years of age, but with pipes worn from use, I sang

I sang in echoing screams and shattering cries

sang into my mic of a scope as I eyed it down

sang as bodies dropped before me like dominoes

bandmates fell off stage in dives caught only by the ground

but I was too drugged to care

performers loved drugs, because their art was too beautiful to bear

and I was no different than Elvis himself

I strung my violin against the throat of a traitor, attempting escape

a symphony of his pleas

I spent a lot of time wondering later

why so little their lives meant to me

as I disperse my Mozart in uncanny flavor

and bullets riddle a sonnet

each chorus laced with blood and vomit

I was just a musician

squeezing my art to life

and that was just reality

that painful and deadly art could be

66

THIS IS AMERICA

This is America

the red white and blue of meaningless hues

a world of freedoms our forefathers paved

that never last

the liberation deliberately slaughtered

This is America

the tarot card readings predict mass hysteria

This is America

where people walk around like

I'm offended by this, I'm offended by that

then bleat a string of slurs in a jumble of facts

because I'm not the one whose offended by that

so cut me some slack

This is America

corporate suits shackle the populus

art is no longer a monolith

the craft to be disassembled and staffed

This is America

where we throw each word down the rifle's spiral

then shove that rifle down another rifle's spiral

until the pyre starts to smother under bodies burden

This is America

we are the sworn in servants of born in

This is America

cauterize the wound with lemon droplets

peel these staples off and watch the city cop it

This is America

67

POETRY

She said

I never understood your poetry

I said

neither did I

until the day I met you and the words just fell in line

LIP RING

We're talking, but I'm not really listening

and there's a spark between us

but what does a spark really mean?

That we're cosmically inclined to be together?

Or like we happened to be at the right place, right time

within the perfect constellations to be temporary lovers

Lovers? What fragmented fractals fly out of the word

when sex sells, but sells what?

More sex? Until our heads explode, and we're left to wonder what's next?

We're stuck, and there's a spark between us

but instead of acting on it, I'm sitting here

pondering what a spark even is?

Instead of spending those precious seconds

memorizing the endless fractals that pierce your eyes

Piercings? You're impaled with piercings,

that mark the beautification of self-mutilation,

the same that got me to you in the first place.

I used my exes as piercings

to cover up the damaged bits that knew they'd never love themselves,

and now I'm staring at your lip ring

wondering if maybe this is the spark,

as in THE spark.

You're pierced,

your ears, your nose, your mouth,

you're perfect, I'm only practice.

Sometimes, in other people

I search for the parts of me I can't show myself,

so tonight kiss me like you know how to die,

let your hot breath

be cooled by your lip ring,

though this won't be your first kiss.

You already gave away your first,

so I'll have to settle for your best,

We're talking, but I'm not really listening

and there's a spark between us.

69

SCAR ON THE MOON

I have thrice looked into those eyes

expecting some grand gesture but

was instead met by nothing of interest

no breathless last cause

with impact to the plot

no loud fireworks

just a fade to black

a black not worthy of art

a black not caring of anything

I have thrice seen your nothing, World

please take it back

I am the exact moment you left me

down to the second

nothing has happened since

it's been a month

and I question myself daily

if I thank God or curse him

that you've never touched this new body

I am not one but every piece

leading up to you

seemingly strung out between the

sinews and synapses to shake the sense

once more

I have thrice entered nothing

three times

three

70

SALE ON HALF BAKED GRADUATES

Mortar board, cranium explored

circuit boards clash with the perpendicular sword

twelve years of gaining for the empty pot to fizzle

hot off the grill of helicopter stuck in perpetual tailspin

twelve years of mailed in, that pale in comparison

to the sheer scale of the overarching braille tale

so set sail to fail until the soul passes through the veil

When every mile is wading through mystic winters

and every second is ticking time off winners

still marinating seconds in Chewbacca defense suiters

cast aside balladmonger cannon fodder

Sam I am

I am not content here or there

I am not content anywhere

always trapped within these same shifts

saying one day ours will be the drill

that pierces the alien spaceships

until that day gravity gradually pulls soul groundward

The progeny of a standardized system

equated to torture by its own creator

and condemned until his last breath

the bloody handed perpetrators

of an alien assimilation

the mind's eye is simply a disguise to the third blind

visualizing those tailored to the design of mediocracy

by snake in Janus like pose

that strikes up comfort from one head

while spitting fear from the other

School doesn't teach us to be kings

it shoves a knife in our crowns

then begs us to thank it

so we can substitute our kids in for another round

I stand not as revolutionary

or self indulged prophet

but rather as a concerned individual

witnessing the death of a civilization that values art

and replaces it with quick returns

Spent the last year surrounded by runway planes

discussing plans for after fact

me, my plans are periodically sawing myself in half

mental state the burdened rock forced to constrain Prometheus

mineral deposit rides the half-life to crap

SATURN

He lays himself onto the road

slipping into the pavement as he dissolves

frequently picking up new limbs

and swapping them with those he had before

he enters a state of metamorphosis

eyes fading away

his essence baked into his tongue

ROAD SIDE SOUL SALE

We're just masses of the barely living

chasing dead man's power

wallets filled with corpses

coffins full of power

a secret service for the makers

a hundred years later

who make us worship banks

and makes us cutthroats to our neighbors

too busy crying over spilled milk

to feed the starving cows

too busy interpreting the universe

to change it for a while

and tell the Greeks they can keep their ivory towers

we've got paper coliseums that we pay for by the hour

for whom we sell our souls as vouchers

dressed in postmodern slave attire

hardwired to be thankful

that we're shackled by the dollar

and whipped by corporate owners

a god with manlike power

an oncoming apocalypse every other half an hour

73

EMMA

I wish I could explain

how fireworks just aren't enough

after looking into your eyes

while you talk about your passions

it's stupid, it's Star Wars

it's something I have no interest in

and yet when you flash that smile

I crave nothing more than to scour

every crevice of every detail

to make your obsession my own

I've never wanted to be someone's passion more

I wish I could explain

how every star in every universe

every beautiful, iridescent thing

could fade instantly and I wouldn't care

so long as a single spotlight illuminated

your gleaming lips

as they wax poetics

in a casual string of jargon

because as I force my art

through pain and booze

you create yours simply by being

so when I write it may not be to cheering crowds

but it's to you

and that's all that matters

CURLY

Her hair weaved in and out of itself

in an endless bird's nest

a tumbleweed of tangled knots

that cascades so elegantly down her back

a great brown river, its tributaries free to roam

over the lanky frame it grew from

she wore herself like the skin was meant for her

which I guess in most people it is

she's constantly developing new skin

to better match her internal cogs

that spin to a mesmerizing beat

a comforting, calming calamity

GLITTERING TRASH MOONS

What if everybody in this world is useless

and we don't have any uses

for the bruises from self abuses that cue in

when the yellowed nooses hang from spruces

What if the self made mountain climbers

have never reached summit

because there is no summit to speak of

What future is there

for a man who spends half his life dreaming of grandeur

and the other expecting failure

What if all life does end with my story

and this metaphysical fantasy crumbles

such as the closing of the back cover of a book

or game paused never to be continued

the characters left striking idle poses

code gone unnoticed until the enclosure closes

Though I doubt the future will be lost without me

which selfishly plagues my withered thoughts with hollowness,

I embrace the literature club's fourth dimensional heralding

perfectly mirroring my mind's repeated strife,

Perhaps I am the NPC craving more

or perhaps I exist within world tucked within a random hurt locker

even with this pen I can't write love into my reality

Nor grant myself a bridge towards happy ending

as happiness is simply the after thought of success

The only people who consider themselves successful

are the ones who crave nothing more

I will be successful the day I die and not a day before

76

BURIED AS A MAN (AN ODE TO BRIANNA GHEY)

I'm begging you to bury me within my own skin

not this fucking cage of binary sin

the skin that gets to breathe, to live, to feel

to carry on to life expectancy

that gets the privilege of such luxuries

as natural causes

and gets to be

the me I see within my head

not the tainted me

the me built on bounds of fear

of hate, of vitriol

or of idealized fantasies, whispered in sexual corners

I'm begging you to bury me within my own grave

not some hole marked by another name

and I can still recall seeing someone like me

old and gray, and thinking

I didn't know we got to live that long

a martyr just to be called by my name

a body crafted of pitfalls and other trappings

trip wires and desperate desires

to wear skin that finally matches

when my real identity is missing between poetry

and scraping myself off bathroom walls

let me exist

I'm begging you to just let me exist

to be buried, not as a man

but as me

I'm begging you to bury me within my own grave

77

AMERICAN DREAM

This is to the country

who needs trauma counseling for their day jobs

we're all trauma

we who rely, on AKs and relays, heroin overdoses just to feel

what they've been starved of since birth

when it's save the children, until it's time to ban the guns

when it's spare the mother only if she has the funds

trauma inherited from mothers and fathers

like eye color

when they give the boy whose mentally ill

a single pill

then monopolize the military unit on a free space

when self destruction is the new sex

and sex is the old model of an outdated consumerist state

Which flag do you bear, is it red? Is it white?

rid the blues like orchestrated hues

this is to the country

who pollute their streets with tanks and guns

then pays for it by raising the price of insulin higher

until insulation become segregating life from imagination

irritation of the eyes, the third blind

feed the pigs their rinds, then praise them for cowering behind

the same guns that kill teenagers

for the simple crime of adjacent skin

this is to the country

that can never stop falling asleep

at the wheel of the American Dream

for fear of the machine, stopping even long enough to cure disease

78

SELF SOUL COMMENTATION

Inside the wheels of crooked spoke spinning

another skirmish of self-soul commentation

where the spokesman's high as hell, lost in thought

spitting slurs into the mic and sipping silver

locked in a burning room with a poltergeist of past

a preliminary of pen smith padlocked

paddling through the loch of games as his mind gains

speed and gravely ganders into the growing ground

outside the windshield as he plummets, panics

as the planes pilot huffs paint in the corner

pulls and prays as the crowd cries over his coffin

silvery moonlight slipping to the commentators skin

before he's sealed away on shelves of self soul

commentation, collective thoughts cancering minds

converging on canvas of internal sins collared,

constrained to never be released as to assume

everything is fine while fantasizing fanatic facilitating,

fronting feels but until that day I'll be stuck

within my mind performing

self soul commentations

79

ME AND HER AGAINST THE WORLD

All my life it's been me and her against the world

wading through all the damage that life hurled,

just me and her against the sky

so when it falls we become Atlas to reunify

to hold the weight of the world, we need only to try

all my life it's been me and her against the sea

that does push its froth with all anger that be

squeezing, condensing, you and me

but such as carbon squeezes to be crystalized diamonds, we will be

strong and steady, always ready, like oak of mighty tree

all my life, it's been me and her against the earth

from point of death back to point of birth

a miracle that every day sprouts new leaves unearthed

till the day that heaven and hell collide into war

it's me and her against the pain

me and her against the tears

me and her against the world for countless years

80

MIRROR OF DAYS TO COME

The old man's eyes reflected years of pain

stress wearing into his wrinkles and finding refuge in his bags

their slow movement indicating the weight they bore

the old man's mouth reflected years of glee

wide toothless grin worn with folds from years of exposure

radiating a love only one with so many years could show

the old man's body reflected hardship

each painstaking movement eating away at the clock

robotic in its minimalism to keep from tiring

the old man's expression flooded with longing

staring at the walls of pictures for flashbacks that hardly remain

remembering a time where innocence was still found

the old man's life is a road map

every little detail, every feature finding some new tale to tell

and I studied it

studied what I would become

what I wanted to become

the old man that would cultivate me to bring forth new legacy to the name we both
bear

81

FIREWORK FACELIFT

Her face is fireworks

flashing lights that catch my eyes

briefly imprinted upon a glistening moon

her voice caught between

the lead and leading

four letter cages box words I can't express

and her lips pronounce cynic as sanctum

without ever knowing what it's worth

Her eyes are syrup traps that anchor harbors

every glance feels like I'm born again

like I'm seeing the world for the first or last time

like I've met you in every happy thought

years before your face existed in my world

and every time in between

her lips pronounce my name like I'm the only one to bear it

without ever knowing what it's worth

82

FOUR ARMS, FOUR LEGS, TWO FACE

Guess that's why we come in sets

cause we're all biologically impaired

unable to act alone, indivisible

that's why our minds can't stay inside the box

cause none of us are perfect squares

but none of us are diamonds either

dying either, in between breaths

or visits, until we're near

although none of us are circles

false closed loop to circumvent a radius

away from any radical

heart can be a zealot for

but out of uncanny zeal, still finding

the shape right for peg

guess that's why you still shape my thoughts

cause we're both biologically impaired

FRAGMENTED

The memory by itself is delicious

in the sense that my soul itself cannot be

where is the pleasure

that poetry brings

where is that little

lonely sense of purpose

that used to ripple throughout

a child's mind, long forgotten

the waves brought with them separation

and hollowed round my soul

which profusely bleeds, periodically voiding itself

I have often met the evil of living

though I'm entirely unsure I survived the encounter

how else could I infuse

this human soul

to the paper

BEDS FOR PEOPLE
FOR BEDS

She disappears in midnight glow

she's paper thin down to her toes

she disappears and I never knew

she disappeared until she did

she, whose fade from life stretches further than her call to death

me, who breathes the carbon that no longer fills her chest

we washed ourselves of innocence

with miles on our feet

I washed her paper skin and knew

those miles weren't so steep

with every falling branch of hair

the trees outside would sway

and as they whistled I swore I could hear

the notes her coffin would play

she washed herself of innocence

we both knew we'd never know

the trees outside looked different

with the job that they would play

she, whose faded smile cracked in parched decay

me, whose smile faded like the third act of a play

85

URANUS

Shambling, face masked in a veil of cloth

a mock Lazarus sealed in fated tomb

clashing his will against a return to hibernation

actively discarding rebirth as his hands clash the walls

jotting anything of half relevance

in a spiderweb of paintings

nothing will obstruct the eyes of those who refuse sight

nor curdle the tongue of gaping grace

extinguished, fated to become the beast of passing

some want in darker

others hold the flames

OTHER NAMES TO CALL ME

Cinephile, photographer, poet, author

The rotten core of a given name

That lingers around past kins

Or a walking grave to immortalize a family's grief

Diseased, marked, afflicted

Brief spark heralded by a great fizzle

Seventeen syllables resting on never-ending waves of self-disgust

Incapable of change while craving movement

Faceless echo chamber of regurgitated past cyphers

The lingering strand of smoke perforating after the gunshot

Or persisting burn of post toke haze

Shambling corpse heading nowhere,

Woman masquerading in the bloody skin of man

Purveyor of turning marathons to race

3am high with friends capturing the remnants of genuine emotion

Nothing, though, built from something more

87

MY HAIR

In this clambering mess of elongated limbs

and portraiture of sprouting potbelly

with stretched sides, juxtaposed to showcase ribs

a theme carried on in pathetic string of pulled pork arms

stained with numerous imperfections

from years of minor afflictions

legs stretching for miles on end

finally lumping into two flesh stretched canoes

crooked and cocked like canines femur

bound with bruises and mirrored ghosts of past breaks

lead foot, the one that crawled from the grave

but at least I have bushy, silky hair

a face scarred with pinprick pressed connect the dots

eyebrows that fall under truce to bypass borders

and Pinocchio's nose, more an improvised shive

matched only by the neighboring mountainous chin

a misty eyed lobotomy patient

yet I bypass all this with five inches of plastic unsheathed

waste yet more precious seconds to fix a messy mop

because everyone needs something they're proud of

88

STICK N' POKE

I swear the music tasted better

when I was running down your throat

now I hope you choke

smothered by his apathy

cause you were just a stick n poke

embedded in the skin of my thigh

you were smoke, coming from the local factory

objects in the mirror are much closer than they seem

and you were just the stick n poke of my dreams

now all they say is "buddy move on"

but it's so fucking hard

when the sweet of your teeth as they ran down my shaft

hurts much more bitter than your nails down my back

I love that I hate you

cause it means I've changed for the worse

that's the only change sober it's par for the course

you were just a stick n poke

drunken and half assed

you were just a stick n poke

of some old forgotten past

a haiku is not meant to be shared

but owned

so I tied you to the bed frame

now I'm the one tied to the past

I hope he doesn't write about you

like I still do

I hope you choke

smothered by his apathy

89

DOMINOES

You were a desolate hound

tethered to my sleigh

desperately trudging through a starved snow

and I knew this

knew that you loved me

that you'd die for me

and still I let you struggle through the sleet

I didn't lose myself in the longing

I found myself in the waning

You were a suffocating trout

floundering for it's last breath

in a sea of oxygen

and still I let you struggle

knowing damn well I held the pail

over a past lovers head

I didn't love myself in the rising

so I'd find myself in the decaying

You were seventeen syllables

draped into any pattern in a pool infinite

that still never reached your perfect

that I abandoned for a glimmer of her imperfections

still you found nothing but the ghosts of flames within my eyes

a haunting you'd quickly regret inviting

I didn't love for the future

so I could linger in the past

90

CLOSE YOUR EYES AND LISTEN

A crinkle in the room

all that keeps silence at bay

dull, flat hum

that gives only slightly to distant cars

a melody to follow

intermixed with curt ticking

of an overzealous clock

stealing time away to push forward

its endlessly spinning hands

deep and dark if you listen close

deep and dark as it counts down

towards its own nonexistence

A splattering of footsteps every so often

project their opinions from the floor above

carelessly creaking with no particular pattern

a drum to accompany the droning hum

and the ticking of lost seconds

a coating of deep silence and yet

an explosive array of slight variations

yet even now, intermixed in all this

your words still echo throughout my mind

greedily devouring all sounds that enter

unfortunately rattling, endlessly

steady as the hum

grim as the beating clock

and unpredictable as the footsteps

91

DIFFICULT

He's got maggots in his teeth

he's got spiders in his hair

y'all beware

he's got worms in his kief

he's got roaches in his lair

y'all beware

Folks say he's difficult

makes mountains out of prairies

fuck the mole hill

he's an elaborate maze of bread crumbs

so he crop circle ants just to minotaur their paths

even his shadow walker bunnies

live longer than your Odyssey

his eyelid scratched stories rival the length of Marienbad

but still no hand, he craft until the bitter end of brittle bread

through seeked mouth hides atomic wonderland

which walks disillusionment down path of Hildebrand

he thinks he came to milk the can

so do not compare him to the Gunsmoke

he's teetering off the barrel of a blunt choke

losing will if you must know

smith if it must blow

ouroboros chains, he hula hoops the same

garage band in DOOM's basement

been a nomad since eight

won't eat the bread off his plate

would rather sit and complain

about how each day is the same

cancel plans just in time to cancel other plans

He's got maggots in his teeth

he's got spiders in his hair

y'all beware

he's got worms in his kief

he's got roaches in his lair

y'all beware

Folks say he's difficult

makes mountains out of valleys

fuck the alley

an appetite for epithets

with an emphasis on empty threats

an epileptic neon test

epitomizing blanket thoughts

and pillow talks

a constant need for overstimulation

you're spitting fools gold, he's rubies

bounce off Rupi's, valor to the newbies

even his throwaways outgun your prestige

a little Aes on the rocks

shaken not cocked

the first shots just to warm the paddle

treat any wandering Goliath just like cattle

his version of a brag

wears a face for a bag

so the man behind the masks

just a man behind another mask

92

UNINSPIRED CLOWN AT THE RAPTURE

I refuse to purge the porcelain bird

that pilots the pen into plunder

though pale in design and if plummets

from flight there's no way of gaining power

inspiration a vase so in case of shakes

resting, bravely on thin line of purgatory

only the insane would burn bridges to create

though never to accelerate, the chance we take

when half the bread is sweeter than full plate

gasoline fed, guzzling matches to test fate

a pyromancers main exhibition of a proclamation

never knowing which sensation to sexualize

in rehabilitation, rearing a cliff in dead of night

the pens caped shadow laps the paper

as the clock mimics the dance

shrinking into lost linework mazes

full enough to pry from between the lines

an encyclopedia of hunger in the rawest sense

until, gone unfed, the inspiration dries in sun

like raisin, raising to flatlines summit

until porcelain birds wings no longer spread

cracked to fate

yet another blank paper held up to light of the rapture

93

OVERDOSE

It's almost beautiful

watching the ones you love fade

carefully caressed by a silence,

bottomless and bare

breaking the comfort

I'd be the first of my friends to die

but I will not let my sister's

bury their older brother

so let's walk a little further

let's go on a little longer

oh I will not leave myself

face down in my own bile

I'll roll over

I'll roll over

just one more tab

one more hit, one more slower

but I'll always be the exact moment you left

not a second further

it's almost beautiful

watching the ones you love wither

but I will not let my mother

bury her only child

allow your eyes to kiss the stars

dressed for funerals as they waltz through the sky

94

THE CLUTTERED EMPTY

My mind's a cluttered nuclear fallout

filled with irradiated irrationalities

a double-headed bear, single bodied contraption

a crowded tetris track of words stacked

or free to roam in herds

or desperate game trails no longer tread upon

that wither and whine in attempt

to once again mold cold words to their surface

My mind's a circular peg down a square gullet

just to asphyxiate this affixed fate

I'm not refusing to write

I'm just slowly farming sentience on my stale plate

I'm just attempting to form solid thoughts

out of this cacophony, a muddied mess of mandolins

played by millions of mannequins

I'm harboring the mantle of the mall they muffled

meanwhile driving my elastic coffin off the cliff

95

NO LOVER

There is no greater grounding than to hold you

no greater comfort than my gentle greed

you walk with no walls around you

a casually, yet casualty, still no lover to me

There is no greater fear than how I found you

reflecting off the ire of a thousand dying stars

how lucky I to be around you

planting fruit around your footsteps

like you were some kinda God

a catastrophe, metastrophe, still no lover to me

There is no greater ailment than your pirouetting lips

I walk with no comfort, nor bodily autonomy

stuck to a skin I'll never be free

these demisexual tendencies

the more you give, the more I need

So casually, a casualty, still no lover to me

but your heart was like a chorus

in the concaves of your chest

Mine the building to a verse

and we both know the rest

but still no matter how much I see

you're still no lover to me

96

MIDWEST OCCULTIST PLAYGROUND

Lightly, slowly, deconstruct

lightly, slowly, deconstruct

lightly, slowly, deconstruct

stamp tongue, mail him out to postal

half hour later newbie surface

to round the clock spiral service

finger groove spoons for passage throughs

wider views, surrealness blooms in color hues

lightly, slowly, decompose

each sensation flounder into follywork

tilt head to Lucy in the sky with dying eyes

and colors he never heard before

that spring through the rising floor

each nirvana closer to overdosing on zen

spinal tap 11, he kick it past the 10

listen soldier, direct lyrics shoulder disorder

lice swarm, devour, various life forms encountered

little self destructions linger just a little longer

in the faces of the formerly further

lightly, slowly, departure

little self deities, litter selective diatribes of passing eyes

labor sucks, drive away, hiring yesterday (oh yay)

later suspicious drug tests and piss scans

but for now he kick the can

less sobriety dependent, more soul seeking saunters

lightly, slowly, drop dead for 16 hours

97

CETACEAN STRANDING

The ocean parts before me

separating the flow of the

current

with my hands

Which offers little resistance

against

me

the flux of the waters surface

billows in slight waves

I can only bend

the water

slightly

never deepening my onslaught

past the reach of extended wrists

Thirsting,

lusting,

throat torn from parch

which the brine does nothing to sooth

the offing,

offering ironic twist

surrounded by this plain of pure water

I crave nothing more than a drink

98

HAIRCUTS AND RAZOR BLADES

He's pastiche, he's spitting through his broken teeth

he's empty cheeks that swallow tongueless underneath

corroded sheath, molding his brain into the folding chair

in the town where razor blades count as commodity

idolize the mouthless face that screams into eternity

with railroad wrist straps, mismatched to the fire

reflected in the iron

he chicken pox, connects the dots for momentary bliss

over tethered arms and webbed toe fillings

he's screaming through an empty face

he tried the "s", it didn't take

he's swinging for the other gate

he faded out the "e" for "t"

he spliffs a second slit

his pen strokes crack vein so meticulous

he festers in the simpleness

he breaches passion briefly

99

SKIN SHEDDING

Start to breathe, I'm starving now

cut off skin, I'm falling now

cut off skin, I'm bleeding now

cut off skin, I cannot breathe

I cannot breathe within this skin

these borrowed arms from mannequins

these yellowed gnarled broken limbs

the floor a bed or susurrus

I cannot breathe, my eyes go dark

my skin dampens, numb the parts

inhale through abandoned lungs

bite the tongue, its falling off

I exit skin, it's nothing now

I breathe in blanks, no breathing out

stops the pain that circles round

return the pinpricks to the skin

that sentience lost from within

cut off skin, I cannot bleed

only touch the ground

FREUDIAN SLIP

My minds sporadic, raised on Illmatic,

slip it under the matt, I'm back at it,

trying to work in the line,

that brings my life meaning,

juggling meth addicts at math practice,

meanwhile prostituting my mind for these lines,

these banshees that scream within the pen,

there's no use trying to silence them,

so I scream their pleas, a hydra disease,

for each line I slay, two more must be written

I think my hair is thinning,

there's no way of rekindling what I envision,

minds a time bomb,

so tic-tock, the thought ran up the clock

but motivation died halfway, and the mouse dropped

the king of poetry is a roadside drunk,

and me? The casualty of verbal warfare,

only I can hear,

perhaps Usain Bolt can foot race life, but not I,

so I rely on art to catapult by,

even livelihoods can be built on the foundations of depression,

so layer stack closure,

until the darkest dreams are bound in leather

NEPTUNE

A shifter cloning the laugh of his creator

from formless ambles that elicit no response

less a soul searcher more a body left to shamble

a foam that leaks out of its many pores

that melt into the air in swirls

he is blind

a cornered animal mutilating the hand that feeds it

return to creation

birthed through destruction

in shedding skin he finally sees his own face

a hero of a thousand tongues

speaks his first few lines

as the earth reclaims her shackles

ANOTHER DISAPPOINTING PROSE

Punch the keys dammit

find something, anything to pull from

any drop of blood left untainted

anything to breed a shred of distinguishable meaning

to an otherwise vacant life

words are, in essence

an isolated, tangible immortality

so drop blood on the canvas until it speckles a masterpiece

don't pull away a second sooner

no matter how much it hurts

no matter how much you want to scream

with the deafening crash

of seventeen syllable intervals

please write

I want the pages to fucking love me

I want the words to fall daft and dim

beneath my grin

I want the pen to fucking fear me

I want the world to fucking love me

in truth that's all I ever wanted

someone to notice I was here

punch the keys dammit

pretend for a single second

that anything I say matters

throw away years of therapy to conjure up the perfect feat

punch the keys dammit

103

STARVED DESIRE

Your touch still a permanence to my desire

your body, weak to my grasp, lingering within me

your caustic mouth erupting flames between moans

pleasure that slides roughly against agony

awaiting the tongue of your master

and the scratches, the scratches, the scratches, the scratches

that carve both backs of this endlessly entangled beast

a great tree that wraps itself inward, branches stumbling against one another

and knots placed haphazardly around a stubborn frame

shedding all identities to the starving floor

as I rip your clothes from your stark frame

such divine bareness in its frothing push against mine

only stopping to breath curses at a God fallen before you

as we both ascend to their position

104

FIND ME

Find me a light and I will consume it

the way Van Gogh consumed paint

in such a way to hide my suicide

in the pursuit of gold through alchemy

Find me a dark and I will smother it in light

caught between the seams of open arms,

that wish for nothing more than to bleed

a blighted light that casts a new reality on the wall

Find me your voice

and within it I will shed my mortal mantle

becoming merely a poet, a translator of your heavenly shouts

while finding my true humanity speckled between syllables

Find me you, and you'll always find me

like a tree finds the soil in that gentle caress,

of roots that tether the ground

or like that tree finds the air, in copious freedom

Find me a rock and I will erode it in your frame

a word and I will chisel it to describe you

a paint brush and each stroke will capture

a monolithic attempt at replicating your features

Find me a god and I will speak not their name

as my final breaths dawn upon me,

but yours, in every sense of the word

as sensations slip around a still tongue of salvation,

Find me

in all future lives

in every second spent together

in every atom that separates us, find me

105

ADOPTED NAMES

He does not wish to be a common man

so he stands, jots through Paine these words of common sense

he's commonly corrected in his daily stance

so he ran this dance with insecurity

and cheated on her with circumstance

now he never takes the chance

to put out his neck

in fear of mangling the dangling breeze block necklace

so he invents a fairytale of

dissociative identity disorder

marks a pseudonym to capture the mad ramblings

of a power hungry personality, unstrained by feasibility

We all fall victim to the adopted moniker

he's the oddity from the Odyssey

he's Nobody

thusly he goes unnoticed by the tortured blind

he's just a shadow puppet, a deformed imaginative silhouette of hands preference

but this shadow walker bunny

is just the product

of the reflection

of the virgin beast with two backs

he can't stomach the man behind the mask

so he backpedals past the mirror

and scrapes eraser shavings off his past

106

TEN SECONDS BUILD FOREVER

Death is real

there's no metaphor to stack

or hide behind

or poem to make it any less itself

it's those empty seconds right after walking into a room

to find you only to realize you're still not there

it's more in the moments I forget

than the times I remember

it's Herculean, it's Lovecraftian

it's so beyond the word that silence bears its own load

and every time I close my eyes

I'm met by those porcelain globes that

greedily mimic life from within an empty vessel

eyes that linger in the unbroken awe

that saw that great whatever in their last few seconds

such a deep emptiness that movies could never attempt to recreate

that words will never reach

an emptiness that speaks to me whenever I'm alone

but catatonic silence wails

and you no longer fill my air

it's not for learning from or growing out of

but simply just to be there

it's not poetic, there's no meaning

it's not poetic, there's no art in death

it's just there

a single second builds a forever without you

and a forever without the me that had you

as your body transformed into something beyond our existence

I stared into nothing and nothing stared back

a deep empty pit that thrashed out violently

sucking away the essence of everything

death is real

I'm shown death is real

and I'm still here

to love you

A SELF AWARE
SIMP'S STILL A SIMP

Tell me you're happier without me

before I forget the damage my lips can do

when they say how much they love you

SOMETIME WE DIE

I play with my rat in the same cage

she bit off her sisters foot in

both of us acting like the past doesn't affect us

one of us a broken hero, decorated in false flags

the other indistinguishable from the first

I write my draft in the same room

my love and I had sex in

I always made my best art between her moans

both of us forming haikus we'd never finish

crafted in-between each others names

I joke with the same throat

that gasped for air between broken ribs

but all the best words are said between seizures

I play with my rat in the same cage

she bit her sisters foot off in

both of us a bit too old to die way too young

both in cages of various size

so we trained in Stockholm

so at least we'd have a home

sometimes we live

what malicious lies

some time we die

precisely the way to waste paper with every line

109

THE DIVINE FEMININE

Not all men

but one in three women

will have their identities stolen from them

their bodies retooled, their skin repurposed

the bloody handed perpetrators of boys will be boys

men will be men, pigs will be pigs

one of my four sisters

even more of my friends

hundreds of thousands I'll never meet

when women are playthings in the eyes of men with power

Not all men

but one out of 176 million will win the lottery

one out of 3.7 million will be eaten by sharks

one out of 103 will die in a car crash

Not all men

but one out of three women will be sexually assaulted before 18

one a minute, every minute

each time ticking closer to a face I know

men who carry smooth talk like brandy

men who wield charming smiles like forest fires

Not all men

not all nuclear bombs

not all rampaging bulls

not all men

but enough

UNTITLED 2

His auburn eyes caught the light in glorious awe

and his skin matched his eyes

almost as if they had once been parts of a whole

until a white river enclosed around the iris

creating two lone islands

in a process akin to Pangea

a skin dropped from the night and cowled in lightning moss

that patched singularities, fractals of glazed sunlight

his lips, twin peaks over an ashen seascape

torturous in their allure

his beauty an act of defiance against an imperfect world

perhaps we could grow young together

and die even sooner

his cheeks contour so carefully

and

his auburn eyes caught the light in glorious awe

III

NOTHING LEFT
BUT BURNING MEN

I would've capitalized if I weren't so scared of drowning

I would've capitalized if I weren't so scared of capsizing

I would've capitalized on all those pretty little lies

before they burnt to dust, and fatally attracted me like moths and flies

nothing left but burning men

and dead dreams in your pretty little head

how strange it is to see, that you were meant to be with me

since the first time that you

slept

with

him

but then again

there's no you

without

him

or any other past event

that led to your current circumstance

so I will not ask you why you came here

to your final place of rest

though I don't know if it's a haven or your death

if I'm the cancer or the treatment

if I'm your Eden or your Macbeth

cause I've read all of the classics but you never seem to care

and I practice and I practice cause I'm just so fucking scared

of you leaving me

if you were ever me

if I'm incomplete

taking pills on the bedside table to calm my shaking anger

But your still asleep

and I just wanna have a conversation

about anything truly

impactful

something to make you truly

notice me

but everywhere I look there's

nothing left but burning men

and dead dreams in your pretty little head

When we met you told me that you wished you were dead

so I decided to love you

until I wished I was dead

I was always scared you'd hate me

so I hated myself

so you wouldn't have to

I'm so scared that this is all I'll ever be

just your

temporary

nothing left but burning men

and dead dreams in your pretty little head

112

THAT WHICH ENDS

I fear not that which ends

only that which never has the chance

to begin

113

NIGHTLIGHT

Hickey canvas

Jackson Pollock pelvis

clawed back like a flog post

shackled like a backstage act

fuck me till I replace myself

chase my hands up your ribs

a race neither of us will win

cause baby we're a Greek mess

getting guilty in the bathroom

knowing there's no recovery in relapse

be the type of girl every good breakup songs about

I'll thank you when I'm sober

but you're the worst detox by far

maybe the dreams not to get romantically dry

but relentlessly high

so let's play make believe, swallow cardboard percocets

and pretend we aren't gonna hate each other

in a year's time

with a love like cold steel

but who would rather die by their own sword?

for now stand on the edge of the world with me

watching time stop

chase my hand up abandoned roller coasters

and clench it once we've reached the top

fuck me on a railway

to the rumble of oncoming trains

and climax only when the combustion sears rosy flesh

give me some sick sense of feeling

114

About the Author

I'm just a weirdo who constantly measures mantras between 'in omnia paratus' and 'memento mori.' I love puzzlework poems and songs that require research to decipher the full meaning of turning poems into games of their own meaning. I am the author of CALL TO THE VOID DEFINITIVE EDITION and SLEEPING AMONG WOLVES. I am excited to share with you the second attempt at my first poetry collection!

I would like to extend a sincere thank you to anyone that has picked up this messy, uncomfortable fraction of my soul. The poems you'll read are an accumulation of years of work. Of the worst days of my life and of the best. Each one means so much to me and I hope they'll strike a chord with you as well, providing levels for you to extract your own meaning and place them into your life whenever necessary.

With each person who reads my book, that is helped along in their own journey by a handful of words I have to say, my purpose is fulfilled a bit more. Remember to never stop fighting, for you or your art, as we all struggle for our own sense of permanence. And again, thank you!

www.ingramcontent.com/pod-product-compliance
Lightning Source LLC
LaVergne TN
LVHW041215080426
835508LV00011B/962